whatever says mark

Knowing and Using Punctuation

by
Terry Collins

illustrated by
Russ Cox

PICTURE WINDOW BOOKS
a capstone imprint

Mark Monday was a quiet baby.

Is he asleep? I think he's asleep.

He's awake. See how he's looking at the ocean? He loves the water!

His older sister, Cleo, was not.

ARRRGH! Run! Here comes Squidzilla!

No one can save you now, city! Bwah-ha-ha!

So, Mark's parents waited ...

Whaaaaaaa!

and waited ...

and waited some more.

6

No matter how much his parents begged, Mark stayed silent.

Until one day at breakfast, Mark spoke.

7

As the years passed, Mark grew ...

but his love for play did not.

His father tried everything.

Sports were not the answer.

Nor was a pony ride.

Mark didn't even yell while riding
the Rattlesnake Rustler.

The Rattlesnake was the fastest
roller coaster in the world.

Mark refused to use punctuation.

No apostrophes.

You don't like me.
You really don't.
I don't get it.

No periods.

Fine. Be that way.
See if I care.

No question marks.

Not even a
single question?

No commas.

None at all, zip,
zero, zilch.

No exclamation points.

But I'm Cleo's favorite!

He did not use punctuation
at the dining room table.

He did not use punctuation
when he hurt himself.

He did not use punctuation even when forced to join Cleo's tea parties.

On the first day back to school,
Mark sat on the bus and worried
about second grade.

He remembered last year.
First grade was tough.

He did not want to read aloud.

He did not like writing sentences.

Most of all, Mark dreaded meeting his new teacher. He was afraid she would make him use punctuation. And he simply had no use for it.

I've heard you're not a fan of punctuation. Is that right? Don't you want people to hear what you have to say?

Well, without the question mark, we can't ask questions. How can we learn any answers without questions?

We can't make a list of our favorite things without commas. We can't even say "can't" without the apostrophe!

Punctuation allows us to write down our address or share the date of our birthday.

The exclamation point lets us yell when we're excited. **Brilliant!**

Without punctuation, we can't tell people what we need or want. We can't explain how we feel.

"Hike it, Dad! Hike, hike!"

"Giddy-up!"

And at that moment—for the first time ever—Mark Monday understood why punctuation was so important.

21

When Mark got home from school that afternoon, things were different ...

and would stay
different from now on.

About Punctuation

Words help us express what we think and feel. But without punctuation, our ideas and feelings can get jumbled up. People might misunderstand what we're trying to say.

Punctuation is a set of marks that make written language clear. Five of the most commonly used marks are periods, commas, apostrophes, question marks, and exclamation points.

. **Periods** end sentences that make a statement. For example: Cleo is a loud little girl. A period tells us to stop.

, **Commas** separate three or more things in a list. For example: Grandpa has white hair, blue eyes, and yellow teeth. We pause when we see a comma.

' **Apostrophes** help make contractions—two words that come together to make one word. Apostrophes take the place of the missing letters. For example: I'm (I am) flying! They also show when something belongs to someone. In this case, they're usually followed by an "s." For example: Those are Mark's cookies.

? **Question marks** are used when asking questions. For example: Are those Mark's cookies?

! **Exclamation points** end sentences that contain strong feelings. For example: Those are my cookies!

That's it! You met Mark, you read his story, and now you know why punctuation is important. What do you want to learn about next?

Read More

Bruno, Elsa Knight. *Punctuation Celebration.* New York: Henry Holt and Co., 2009.

Cleary, Brian P. *The Punctuation Station.* Minneapolis: Millbrook Press, 2010.

Ganeri, Anita. *Punctuation: Commas, Periods, and Question Marks.* Getting to Grips with Grammar. Chicago: Heinemann Library, 2012.

Rosenthal, Amy Krouse. *Exclamation Mark.* New York: Scholastic Press, 2013.

Special thanks to our adviser, Terry Flaherty, PhD, Professor of English, Minnesota State University, Mankato, for his expertise.

Editor: Jill Kalz
Designer: Lori Bye
Art Director: Nathan Gassman
Production Specialist: Kathy McColley
The illustrations in this book were created digitally.

Picture Window Books are published by Capstone,
1710 Roe Crest Drive, North Mankato, Minnesota 56003
www.capstonepub.com

Library of Congress Cataloging-in-Publication Data
Collins, Terry (Terry Lee)
  Whatever says mark : knowing and using punctuation / By Terry Collins.
    pages cm. — (Nonfiction picture books. Language on the loose.)
  Includes bibliographical references and index.
  Summary: "Introduces five of the most common types of punctuation—apostrophe, comma, exclamation point, period, question mark—through the telling of an original story"— Provided by publisher.
  ISBN 978-1-4048-8318-5 (library binding)
  ISBN 978-1-4795-1917-0 (paperback)
  ISBN 978-1-4795-1904-0 (eBook PDF)
1. English language—Punctuation—Juvenile literature. I. Title.

PE1450.C73 2013
  428.2—dc23   2013008068

Printed in the United States of America in North Mankato, Minnesota.
032013   007223CGF13

24

Internet Sites

FactHound offers a safe, fun way to find Internet sites related to this book. All of the sites on FactHound have been researched by our staff.

Here's all you do:

Visit *www.facthound.com*

Type in this code: 9781404883185

Super-cool stuff!   Check out projects, games and lots more at **www.capstonekids.com**

Look for all the books in the series:

Frog. Frog? Frog!
Understanding Sentence Types

Monsters Can Mosey
Understanding Shades of Meaning

whatever says mark
Knowing and Using Punctuation

When and Why Did the Horse Fly?
Knowing and Using Question Words